police patrol

Publication Number 135
AMERICAN LECTURE SERIES

A Monograph in
AMERICAN LECTURES IN PUBLIC PROTECTION

Edited by
LE MOYNE SNYDER, M.D.
Medicolegal Consultant
Lansing, Michigan

RALPH F. TURNER
Associate Professor of Police Administration
Michigan State College
East Lansing, Michigan

CHARLES M. WILSON
Superintendent, Wisconsin State Crime Laboratory
Madison, Wisconsin

O. W. WILSON
School of Criminology
University of California
Berkeley, California

R. S. FISHER
Office of the Chief Medical Examiner
State of Maryland
Baltimore, Maryland

By

RICHARD L. HOLCOMB

Chief, Bureau of Police Science

State University of Iowa

Iowa City, Iowa

Formerly, Lieutenant and Assistant Director

Kansas City, Missouri, Police Academy

Seventh Printing

POLICE
PATROL

CHARLES C THOMAS · PUBLISHER
Springfield · Illinois · U.S.A.

Published and Distributed Throughout the World by

CHARLES C THOMAS • PUBLISHER

BANNERSTONE HOUSE

301-327 East Lawrence Avenue, Springfield, Illinois, U.S.A.

NATCHEZ PLANTATION HOUSE

735 North Atlantic Boulevard, Fort Lauderdale, Florida, U.S.A.

First Printing,   1948
Second Printing,   1952
Third Printing,   1957
Fourth Printing,   1961
Fifth Printing,   1964
Sixth Printing,   1968
Seventh Printing,   1971

With THOMAS BOOKS *careful attention is given to all details of manufacturing and design. It is the Publisher's desire to present books that are satisfactroy as to their physical qualities and artistic possibilities and appropriate for their particular use.* THOMAS BOOKS *will be true to those laws of quality that assure a good name and good will.*

Printed in the United States of America

I-1

To Wilma

foreword

WHEN THE SIZE and the importance of the field are considered, there has been relatively little written on police methods and techniques. This is particularly true of the basic police methods. Much of the material that has been written has been concerned with the technical aspects of the problem or has dealt with phases of primary interest to the administrators. The officer on the beat, doing the day-by-day job that is the backbone of law enforcement, must depend almost entirely upon experience and the advice of older officers. These methods of learning are excellent, but are of necessity a slow process. They can well be supplemented by printed material.

This publication was written with that in mind. This is the first of a series designed to present the methods used in everyday police work. The material was drawn from the experience of many police officers in scattered sections of the country. The methods presented are intended to apply to police patrol everywhere, but more particularly to motorized police patrol in cities and towns.

It would not be possible to acknowledge each officer who assisted in assembling this material since points presented were learned from a great number of individual officers and since at least 20 police officers read and commented on the material before publication. I am certain, however, that they will gain satisfaction from seeing their suggestions in writing.

The illustrations are by Robert W. Gadbois and Harold Schwarm.

R.L.H.

Iowa City, Iowa

contents

police patrol

introduction

THE POLICE PATROL, whether on foot, in an automobile, or on a motorcycle, is the basic law enforcement method. While it is not as spectacular as the many interesting and valuable laboratory techniques, and lacks the glamour of shadowing or investigating, it gets the job done. Careful patrol by intelligent officers is the first line of defense against crime. The man on the beat does the day-by-day work that makes or breaks a law enforcement agency, that controls the vast majority of criminals and is the major basis of the police function of the protection of life and property and service to the public.

Many officers will find patrol duty monotonous. This is the fault of the officer, rather than the fault of the duty. Patrol is monotonous if the officer is only trying to put in eight hours on duty while walking or driving around the area assigned to him. On the other hand, patrol can be extremely interesting if the officer tries to do a good job. In patrol work you are dealing largely with people. The study of individuals is one of the most interesting things in the world. If the officer on patrol duty attempts to analyze his area, the people in the area and their problems, he will find that time goes faster and he is doing a better job. No matter how dead a beat may seem, there is a great deal to be observed if the officer is really looking for it. Each area has its own

3

Patrol is the first line of defense against crime

characteristics and its own police problems. The success of the officers assigned to this area will depend on how well they study the area and then apply police methods to solution of police problems. Much of the monotony often associated with patrol work will disappear when the officer makes an intelligent effort to discover and solve these problems. This is not easy work. It takes a great deal of thinking, and thinking is one thing that many people avoid. But it must be noted that the successful people in this world think. Men are set apart from animals by their ability to think. An officer who patrols his beat without thinking or doing a minimum of thinking is not setting himself very far apart from an animal and he could very well be replaced on his beat by an intelligent police dog.

From its very name patrolling is not pleasant. The word comes to us from the French "patrouiller," meaning "to go through puddles." This is an excellent basis for the word, for good patrolling means going through puddles, and through garbage-filled alleys, up rickety back stairs, through snow and sleet and rain, day and night, winter and summer. The criminal can choose the time he wants to work, and so he often chooses a time when he believes the police are not alert, or hanging around the station out of the weather. Police patrol must be continuous and alert.

your uniform and equipment

BEFORE YOU START *on duty check your uniform and equipment.* Make sure that it is in top shape and that you have everything. Many police departments make a practice of inspecting the men before they start on patrol. Even if your department doesn't hold an inspection, make sure that you could pass the most rigid check by a commanding officer. If you are going to be a good police officer, look like a good police officer.

Your uniform must be clean, well pressed and in good repair. Police duty is very hard on uniforms and if you have to buy your own, it is difficult to keep up a uniform, particularly on the salaries that police officers are paid. However, there's no excuse for letting your uniform be dirty, unpressed or in a bad state of repair. You can look respectable in a very old uniform if it is properly kept.

Your brass and all of your leather equipment should be well shined. This not only adds to your appearance, but is an aid to your own safety. If you keep your leather equipment shined, it will last longer and is less likely to break in an emergency. The same is true of your brass. Some police officers neglect the brass catches on their holster or on their shell holder for so long that they are almost corroded shut.

As a matter of fact, keeping your uniform and equipment up saves you a lot of trouble. Everyone, even many drunks, respects a police officer who looks like a police officer. You're going to get a lot fewer arguments. A bum is likely to argue with a police officer who is only a little neater than he is.

your gun

IT IS ONLY GOOD SENSE *to keep your gun in top condition.* This gun is your life insurance. It would seem obvious that every police officer would keep his gun in perfect condition. This is not always the case. A great many police officers clean their gun only when they are forced to. The best gun made will soon deteriorate in police service unless it is properly maintained. If you don't keep it up, you are going to be standing there sometime with just a couple of pounds of iron in your hand instead of a weapon that can really do you some good. *You should not only keep your gun up, but you should know how to use it.* If your department doesn't have regular firearms training, spend a little money for ammunition and learn how to shoot. Don't just buy a box of shells and go out to the city dump and bang away at cans. This sort of practice doesn't do you any good. Get someone who really knows how to teach you, and then when you do practice, make every shot count. You can learn to shoot fairly well after firing only 200 or 300 rounds of ammunition if you have had good instruction and do a lot of dry firing. Once you have learned to shoot, keep in practice. Ten or 20 rounds a week will do this. If you can, fire your gun every day or two. This may be expensive but you may be able to borrow a .22 revolver and practice with it. Your department may have such a gun. This is good practice, even though the caliber isn't as large as your service gun. You should, of course, practice with your service gun but a .22 will help keep you in top form. Incidentally, *if you have to buy your own gun, spend enough money to get a good one.* Most departments have a regulation requiring an officer to carry guns of a certain caliber. This should be uniform. The .38 special is almost exclusively used in police service in this country. The advantage in standardizing firearms means that you can get ammunition from another officer in an emergency and fire his gun as well as your own.

the importance of a notebook

A GOOD NOTEBOOK *and a pencil are almost as important to a police officer as his gun.* The sort of a notebook you carry may depend upon department regulation. Many departments have an excellent notebook system developed for their officers. If your department doesn't have any such system, get a good small notebook of your own. The briefest note is better than the best memory. Some officers think they can remember everything they see and hear on a beat. This isn't true, particularly if the question does not come up until months afterward. Get a habit of making notes on everything you believe you should remember. If you ever do make a mistake in deciding whether or not to write something down, the mistake will be in the direction of not writing it rather than in writing too much. If the department doesn't furnish you the information in some other convenient way, you should keep a record in your notebook of stolen automobiles, wanted persons and such other information as will assist you. In addition, write down information that will assist you in the prosecution of cases. There should be a section for miscellaneous matters. You will get tips, for example, that you will want to remember. *Your notebook should be looseleaf.* This will allow you to purchase a substantial cover and then to remove pages and file them. You should keep your notes indefinitely. It may be that you will want to refer to them years afterward. There is another advantage in the loose-leaf notebook. You can testify in court from your notes taken at the scene of a crime or written down shortly afterward. This is a great help to you. However, if you do use such notes on the witness stand, the opposing attorney has a right to examine your entire notebook. Since your notebook will carry information on many other cases than the one on trial, you should bring in only the notes that apply to the particular case.

Don't forget your flashlight. Even if you are patrolling in the daytime, you should have a flashlight. You never know when you are going into a basement, attic or someplace where there is no light at all. Make sure that the batteries are in good condition and be sure to carry a spare bulb. It is too bad that no one has ever yet developed a good flashlight for police use. All of them wear out too soon. As a result, you have to watch your flashlight constantly to make sure that it is reliable.

Many departments either furnish handcuffs or require the men to carry their own. *If you have cuffs, make sure that they are in working condition and that you have the key with you.* Check the lock and the ratchet on your cuffs occasionally. It is best to lubricate them with graphite rather than with oil. The oil will stiffen up in cold weather and will collect dirt so that your cuffs may not be reliable.

the police club

IF YOU CARRY A BLACKJACK, *make sure that it is in good condition.* The leather and the stitching deteriorates. As a result, you may find that your blackjack is not usable when you need it suddenly. This can be a fatal mistake. There is a difference in opinion upon the actual value of a blackjack. Many police officers feel that if you're close enough to hit a man with one, you are too close for comfort. Again, it is difficult to really put a man out of service with a blackjack unless you hit him in the head. This is never a good place to hit anyone unless they have committed an offense for which you could kill them. Such a blow can be too dangerous. Many departments have put a great deal of emphasis upon the use of the club. *A good night stick properly used can be an excellent weapon.* You can disable a man without causing any permanent injury, and at the same time you do not need to get near enough to put yourself in danger. You can also block a variety of blows or kicks with your club. If you carry a club, know how to use it. Never lift it back to hit anyone. They can come in and take the club away from you before you know what has happened. The best way to carry your club is with your hands firmly grasping each end. If anyone grabs the club, you have leverage since your hands will be outside of his. You can take the club away from him and are in a good position to hit. The best blow with a club is to hit on the side of the knee joint. This sort of blow can knock a man down and be extremely painful without being dangerous. From the basic position described, you can work even a 24-inch club in very restricted quarters. Remember though, never hit a man in the head with a club unless you intend to kill him. If you do have to hit around the head, hit the junction of the neck and the shoulder. A good blow there will knock a man out, yet is relatively safe. Don't forget that you can be very effective by jabbing with the club. This will give you about six inches additional reach.

theories of patrol

THERE ARE TWO distinct theories of patrol. Both are used by some agencies. The first system is to *patrol so as to attract attention*. Let the criminals, and in-

One system of patrol tries to attract attention, another to avoid attention

cidentally the public, know you are on the job. The very fact that the police are uniformed in a distinctive manner is based on this theory of patrol. Some cities paint their police cars white, to carry out this theory; other cities require the officers to walk always out on the curb. One city went so far, at one time, as to require the officers to walk out in the street so as to be seen most easily. The opposite theory is based on *attracting as little attention as possible.* Under this system, a high proportion of police cars are painted some color other than black, often out-of-state or ordinary license plates are used, officers in uniform walk close to buildings, follow alleys, and try to stay out of sight.

motorized patrol
vs. foot patrol

WHEN POLICE PATROL first originated, the officers were usually on foot. Officers assigned to patrol outside of cities, or to patrol large areas might occasionally be mounted on horse-back. But the patrol system that developed in our American cities starting in the last century, was almost entirely a system of foot patrol. With the advent of the motor car many of the more progressive chiefs of police saw the possibility of a more flexible and faster police patrol. However, motorized patrol is a relatively new technique in police work. A few police departments had motorized patrol wagons soon after the automobile was invented. These were kept at district stations and responded to emergency calls. The actual use of the motor vehicle in a definite patrol area and for the purpose of replacing foot patrolmen did not develop until the 1920's. As a result, motorized patrol has a history of not over 30 years. However, because of the many possibilities of motorized patrol, especially after the advent of radio communication, the use of motorized patrol increased greatly. Some cities went so far as to almost entirely replace the foot patrolmen with patrolmen in squad cars. During World War II because of the manpower shortage on police departments, some police organizations depended entirely upon motorized patrol.

16

This was true even in some of our larger cities.

Both systems of patrol have their adherents. Some police officers will claim that foot patrol is the entire answer, that one good foot patrolman will get more done than a dozen automobiles, and that all of the real police work is done by the man on foot. Other police administrators will claim that the automobile is the final solution. They will say that an alert officer or team of officers placed in a car with two or three way radio can cover more territory and cover it better than a much larger number of foot patrolmen. Here, as in the case of the two general theories of patrol, we find that a combination of the two is probably most effective.

No police administrator should set up a system of patrol without first very carefully studying his problem. One of the best analyses ever made of the patrol problem was made by O. W. Wilson, then Chief of Wichita, Kansas. In the middle 30's Wilson made not only a block study but a building-by-building study of the police problem in Wichita. He rated each block on the basis of the police hazards existing in that block. Then he reduced these hazards to a score, and combining this score as to hazard with the size of areas involved, broke his city down into a number of patrol areas of approximately equal difficulty. All assignments were made on the basis of this study. Wilson's study was unusually thorough. It may be that many police departments will not have the facilities or the budget to make that complete a study. In any case, the principles used here can be applied. If such a study is made it will be found that there are areas where a foot patrolman may be unusually effective, but on the other hand, there will be areas where police officers in automobiles will be the best solution.

do not follow an obvious schedule

LIKE MOST THINGS, the most satisfactory method of patrol is a combination of two extremes; combining the two, using the best of each, parts of both, depending on the situation. Thus, for general police patrol, the best system is to patrol so that every one knows you are on the job, yet patrol so that no one knows where you will be next. A police chief of many years of experience expresses this very well by telling his men to be "systematically unsystematic." That is, do not follow any fixed route or schedule that a criminal might observe, but at the same time see that you cover all of your beat in such a way as to give adequate protection. This is not easy. The easiest way to operate, of course, is to lay out a route and schedule so that you need not think about what you are doing. But remember that while this is the easiest way for you, it is also the easiest way for the criminals. There is nothing they like better than a police officer who is so systematic that they know that he visits a certain point, say the back door of a drug store, every night at, say, 11:36, 12:03, 12:49, 1:32.

Few officers have so little interest or intelligence that they will knowingly use that regular a schedule, but far too many officers have fallen into certain regular habits without realizing it. For example, if

19

Don't help criminals lay out timetables

the last restaurant on their beat closes at 11:30, at 11:15 they will be there for one last cup of coffee. If a train comes in at 1:45, they will meet it to see if any of their friends are on it. If the newspapers come in on a truck at 4:40, they will be there to get their copy. Or again, in driving, or walking around town, certain routes become favorites, maybe to avoid rough paving, perhaps to go by their own home. Criminals are clever in certain ways. They spot these things, so the good officer learns his own faults first, and eliminates them.

develop techniques
to help you patrol

IN ELIMINATING FAULTS, an officer can, at the same time, develop some habits that will improve his patrol and increase his number of arrests. *One such habit is to back-track.* That is, turn around and cover a block, or an alley that you have just covered. Someone may have been waiting for you to get by before he kicked in a door. Turn around any place, in the middle of a block, for example, and go back for half a block or so. This takes time, but it gets the job done. In a car, go around a block twice, perhaps cutting through the alley on the second trip.

Another good system is simply to *step into a doorway,* or some other place where you can see without being seen, and wait for a few minutes, watching carefully. This may fool even the most cautious criminal.

When walking a beat, *do not come down a street for blocks, trying every door and flashing your light at random.* This makes you a set-up for even an inexperienced thief. Remember that he likes nothing better than to know where you are and this is one of the best ways to let him keep track of your every move. While this seems like a practice everyone would avoid, I recall, while I was waiting for an escaped prisoner to show up, watching an officer walk almost six blocks down a business street in this

Drop back into a doorway now and then

manner so that I could observe him for at least 20 minutes. In contrast, he did not notice three of us standing quietly in a doorway until he was within a few feet. This sort of patrol may look good to the casual observer, but it looks foolish to an experienced officer.

No one enjoys walking down a dark alley, littered with trash and bricks; no officer likes to go up broken-down stairs to a loading platform covered with smashed crates and full of holes; spaces between buildings are often narrow, damp or dirty but if an officer is going to do the best possible job of patrolling, he must suffer these inconveniences. *Routes should be selected on the basis of doing the best patrol job,* not on the basis of doing the easiest job. Criminals break in at the point where they believe they have the least chance of being detected. Too often this is a little-used back window in a weed-, brick- and broken-bottle-covered back yard. In addition, this practice allows for the element of surprise. Thieves avoid towns where they know that an officer is likely to step out from between two buildings, or suddenly come out of an alley, or up onto a loading dock.

There are a couple of habits that should be developed for use when entering alleys. The first of these is to *stay near the side of the alley. Avoid silhouetting yourself.* Remember that the fellow in the alley is probably in the dark and if you walk down the center of the alley you will be easier to observe. You may want to walk by the entrance of an alley,

Don't forget the alleys

then turn around and enter the alley, moving along the sides of the buildings. The second point to remember is to wait after you have entered an alley until your eyes become accustomed to the change in light. This will not only serve the purpose of letting you see better in the darkness of the alley, but will give you a chance to observe anyone moving as a result of your entrance into the alley. It is ordinarily easier to see someone moving when you are standing still yourself than it is when you are moving.

know what you are patrolling

A THOROUGH KNOWLEDGE *of the geography of the area patrolled is essential.* A good officer must know every street in his area. He must know, for example, if it dead-ends anywhere, if it is broken by an intersecting block or railroad tracks, and any other peculiarities. He should know its correct name and any odd names it may have had. He must know all of the street numbers and learn any unusual features. Some houses have been misnumbered and never changed. In some towns, new methods of numbering have been put in effect so that any number of variations in street numbers may appear. For example, 608 may be directly across the street from 617 instead of 607 or 609. *Equally as important as the streets are the alleys.* A good officer will be as familiar with them as he is with the streets. You must, in addition, *know all the buildings on your beat,* not only the street numbers, but the name of the buildings, and not only the name in common use but the official name of the building which may be considerably different. The building everyone calls the "Bank" might be officially known as the "Interstate Trust Building." In addition to knowing the location of buildings, an officer must know their internal structure, the location of stairways, doors, how to get to the roof, where fire hoses and extinguishers are located, and other facts of this nature.

You should not only know your streets, street numbers, and location of public buildings for use in finding your own way around, but you should know them so that you can guide citizens. Most people turn to the police as the final answer as to the best way to get to a destination. It is excellent public relations to be able to point out the best way to get to a certain location to not only the natives of your city but to strangers. Remember that most people have little contact with the police. *The fact that you are able to give a citizen a good route to the location he was seeking may be the most effective contact your department will ever have with that citizen.* If you can do a good job he will think you are a good officer and that your department is a good department. On the other hand, if you don't know how to get to that location, if you are brusque and impolite in answering his query, you and your department will fall in his esteem. It should be remembered here that the route you give to a citizen to follow to a specific location might not be the route you would follow yourself. You might follow some complex route because it was actually faster. Inasmuch as possible, *give citizens the simplest directions,* even though it may take them a little further in actually reaching their destination. If you do give complex directions, they may lose their way and blame you rather than themselves. If it is necessary to give complex directions, there are two devices that will assist you. One is to write down the directions or ask the citizen to write them down. The other is to direct the inquirer only part of the way and then tell him a good point to ask directions for the remainder of the trip.

It goes without saying, of course, that *an officer should know the best routes to follow in an emergency*. He must plan in advance so as to avoid such

Anything like this ever happen to you?

hindrances as crowded streets, railroad crossings that may be blocked for several minutes, streets that are impassable in wet weather. If an officer will consider all of the possible routes when he is patrolling, he will be able to choose instantly the quickest and safest route in an emergency. This sounds like too obvious a point to mention; however, I recall a case where a car carrying an inhalator to a drowning went down a narrow street on a Saturday night. The men in the car knew from years of experience that this street, particularly on Saturday night, was filled with double parkers. Traffic jammed up on them and they were delayed, unable to go either direction, for several minutes. On either side of the route they chose were wider and always passable streets. If they had considered, they would have realized that either one was a better route.

know the business places on your beat

BECAUSE MOST BUSINESS PLACES are not occupied at night, they are more frequently burglarized than private homes. Because many of them have large amounts of cash on hand, they are also likely subjects of robberies. Because, in order to sell merchandise, it is necessary to make it easily available to the public, stores are subject to larceny. Therefore, *as business places present a police problem out of proportion to their number, a successful officer will study their problems carefully.*

It is important to *know all of the entrances and exists to business houses,* not only the ones ordinarily used by the public, but the little used and poorly located doors that a thief might note. Learn the location of windows that might be used as means of entrance or exit. Do not overlook the possibility of a thief climbing up to the roof of an adjoining building, then crossing over and coming in through a skylight, or a window. In older buildings there may be doors cut into an adjoining building, but never used. Such doors are easy marks. Consider the possibility of burglars going through a wall from a vacant building, or basement, into an occupied one.

You will learn from experience that certain sorts of business are more likely to be the victims of criminals than others. While the experience will vary from one section of the country to another, it is generally true that restaurants, filling stations, delicatessens, and cigar stores are more frequently held up than most other types of business. Neighborhood grocery stores are very often burglarized, particularly

A roof is a good spot for a break-in

by the younger criminals. Department stores and five-and-ten cent stores seem to be the usual victims of shoplifters. These are only suggestions. Study the experience in your patrol area so you can adapt your patrol to the types of crimes prevalent there.

check protective devices

AN OFFICER SHOULD *be familiar with the protective devices used in business*. He should know the type of locks used, whether or not there are screens or shutters on the rear windows, if there are burglar alarms and, if so, how they operate. He should encourage business owners to keep all of these devices in first class shape and to add to them when necessary.

The argument always comes up that if a burglar wants in badly enough, he will get in no matter what sort of lock or alarm you have. This is true up to a certain point, and in the case of a highly skilled burglar. However, many of our burglaries are committed by relatively inexperienced youths who do not know all of the answers and who won't attempt a place where the physical protection has been well-planned. In any case, even with a skilled criminal, better locks, shutters, bars and other protective devices will slow him down and increase his chances of capture.

Remember that *light is always an excellent protective device*. Even a 15-watt light properly located in a store building will prevent burglaries. A well-located outside light may assist in protecting several business places from entry through their rear doors or windows. Encourage the merchants to place some lights and to let you know about the placement of these lights. The procedure of placing a light where it will illuminate the safe is well known. This general

33

Check the locks and bars on your beat

principle should be kept in mind. In any case, if a light is to be placed, encourage the merchants to put in a good light that will be entirely reliable. They should always replace the light bulbs so that there will not be false alarms as a result of the light being out. A well-located light is also of material assistance in detecting fires. Very often a fire will smoke for considerable time before it breaks into flame. It is almost impossible to see smoke in the rear of a building unless there is some illumination there. The merchants may be able to get the city to place additional lights in the alleys. Often a city will have a favorable contract with the public service company so that the cost of lights in alleys is low. The merchants of the city should be encouraged to investigate this possibility.

know the location
of valuable stock

A GOOD OFFICER will know the location of safes, vaults, important filing cases, valuable or easily sold stocks, such as cameras or cigarettes, narcotics in drug stores, large woolen or silk stocks, or any other valuable items. Certain thieves specialize, or an ordinary thief may receive a good offer for a "hot" item, and you may find some morning that the local drug store lost $1500 worth of vitamin products during the night. You cannot check everything in town, but thefts do follow patterns, so *find out what things are being stolen in your area,* and then find out who keeps them for sale in your town and how well-protected they are.

Stocks of narcotics are very often the subject of burglary. A narcotic addict is totally dependent upon securing morphine or one of the other drugs that he may be using. Addicts will go to extreme lengths to secure these drugs. They are, in addition, exceptionally clever and are more often than not excellent thieves. They will burglarize drug stores, doctors' offices, or doctors' cars to secure narcotics. Almost every doctor's bag that is stolen has been stolen by a narcotic addict. As a result, pay particular attention to these points, particularly if you believe that there are addicts in town. Transient addicts very often accompany carnivals, circuses, or similar organizations. While the larger carnivals and circuses have attempted to eliminate such addicts, travelling with such an organization gives an addict an excellent opportunity to move around the country.

know how to secure the information to do a good patrol job

IF THE LAW *enforcement officers of this country had all of the information regarding crimes that the general public has, they could solve almost every crime committed.* If the police knew the many clues, major and minor, that the good law-abiding citizens of their community knew, but were not disclosing, no criminal could escape arrest. Why, then, do citizens fail to give the police this valuable information? There are many reasons: Fear of being involved in court, fear that their information will not be treated confidentially, lack of confidence in the officer, lack of opportunity, a belief that they may be ridiculed if the information is of no value.

The police can overcome this natural resistance of the public only by careful planning. *The administrators of the police department must build a good police department and then let the public know that they have a good police department.* Equally important, each officer must feel his responsibility. He must realize that he has been selected and trained to protect the lives and the property of the public. This is a great trust and a great responsibility. If an officer accepts this responsibility the public will soon know by his attitude. When the public knows that a man is a police officer and not a glorified night watchman, their attitude toward him will change.

Every witness gets visions of being worked over in court.
They have seen too many movies

They will have confidence in him. They will assist
him in a number of ways. The caution must be
stated that it is not only necessary to look like you
are doing a good job, but it is necessary to really
do a good job. There is no quicker way to fail and
to lose the confidence of the public than to put up a
false front.

know the owners, managers and employees and their habits

IT IS OF REAL VALUE TO *know the usual hours of business of a store and the habits of the employees in relation to working irregular hours.* That is, you

Know the store employees

should know the opening and closing time, the usual lunch hours and how much night or early morning work may be expected. There are several reasons for this. First, many hold-ups occur at the time the first person unlocks a business in the morning, or at lunch time when fewer employees are present or just

41

before closing when, quite often, the amount of money is at a maximum. It is of value to know habits of working outside of business hours so that you can spot unusual conditions quickly. That is, if you see someone at about 8:00 a.m. in a store where no one is ordinarily present until 9:00 a.m., it is time for action. The danger in this is that an officer may be inclined to disregard activity in a store outside of closing hours simply because the personnel often work then arranging stock. This should not be done. Check the store to see who is inside. You may check a store many times without incident and then on the next time, make a good arrest.

Remember that *not all burglars operate stealthily!* Some unusually clever and bold burglars may enter a place, turn on some of the lights, and move stock out just as though they were employees. This is unlikely to occur in the smaller towns, but it has been a method of operation in larger cities. Do not be afraid to check anything that looks out of line to you. Many good arrests have been made because some policeman followed a "hunch."

A good officer will know all of the business owners or managers on his beat and their key employees. He should have some established method of contacting one of them in case of any emergency such as a burglary or fire, or in case a window or door is found open or unlocked. In addition, knowing these persons will allow an officer to make a quick check of any place of business occupied outside of the usual hours.

Some of the better police departments systematize all of the information covered above by making up a card for each business. On one side of the card may be a drawing of the store with door, windows, skylight, location of electric lights, alarms, safes, valuable stocks, etc., drawn in, and on the other side, the names, addresses and phone numbers of the owner, manager, principal employees and any special note regarding the business. The police value of such a record is obvious, and the public relations value of this system should not be disregarded.

check the danger spots

EVERY PATROL AREA *has locations where trouble is likely to develop.* These points may be taverns, pool halls, hotels, railroad stations, rooming houses, penny arcades, or parks. It is a good plan to spot your police car and have one officer get out and walk through the place. This will only take a few minutes but it will have its effects. It will not only prevent much trouble from developing but will give you an idea of who is around. Criminals and trouble makers of all sorts congregate in these places. They don't like to see the police come in and they may avoid these locations. While this may only mean that they move to some other spot, if they move often enough, they may get the idea and move to another town where the police department isn't as efficient. I know that the philosophy of shoving off your problems to another town isn't the best, but remember that they aren't going to the towns that have good police departments. This sort of patrol work helps you to learn the people that you are going to see in trouble. You will get to know a great many of them by appearance or by name. As a result, when you want to pick them up for something, it will be a lot easier for you to spot them. When you use this system, you will always have a good chance of picking up a wanted person or a run-away. Run-away children very often will be found in railroad or bus depots or around penny arcades or similar locations. If you

44

are familiar with the usual hangers-on at these places, a stranger will stand out and it isn't too difficult to find out who he is.

This plan also gets you familiar with the lay-out of such places. As a result, when you have to go into one of them in a hurry, to get someone or to break up a fight, you will know your way around. You will not only know the usual entrances or exits but the back ways out. The seconds you save by knowing this will determine whether or not you will be able to make an arrest.

A number of places you visit in this way and the frequency with which you visit particular places will depend upon the problems that they present. It may not hurt to drop into certain taverns several times a night, if they have been causing you trouble. The owners won't like it and may complain to your superiors. However, you have good reason for going in and your commanding officers will support you.

When you do make a check on such a place, do not overlook any law violations. Don't fall into the habit of simply walking through the place without really seeing anything. If you see a drunk in a tavern, arrest him. It is a violation of the law. It is always a good practice to check for proper licenses. The usual licenses in any city do not cost a great deal, but in spite of this many proprietors of places of business that cause you trouble are likely to do a little chiseling. They will avoid buying all the licenses they should have or they will let a license run expired for some time before renewing it.

get acquainted with the public

IT IS UP TO *the police to gain the confidence of the public*. Let merchants, residents and all other people you come in contact with know that the police are out to help them and can be trusted. To do this, as a police officer, you must have a sincere desire to help the public. You can't put up a false front. Take an interest in a merchant's business. Everyone likes to talk about the way he makes a living. In talking with merchants, however, two things must be avoided. First, avoid giving the impression you are just loafing around his place. Talk with him as long as it does not interfere with your duties and as long as you do not interfere with his business. Second, do not appear to be telling him how to conduct his business. You may know more about it than he does, but he still runs the business. However this does not mean you should not make suggestions that are in line with your duties as a police officer. Suggest improvements in protection, showing how a door or window may have been overlooked, how a night light would help prevent burglaries, how a door might be made safer by putting on a dead lock. This is all valuable as a matter of public relations. In addition, officers might call on the merchants to warn them of persons passing bad checks and counterfeits, or working some other racket, and ask the merchants to call them at any time and for any reason where they believe police can help. Suggest

46

that they bank frequently, that they keep money in the cash register down to a minimum, that they be careful in moving money from place to place in the store and avoid any regular pattern of handling cash that might be observed. Suggest that they work out a

This system may let you know if there has been
a break-in

system with you that would show if any intruder was in the place of business after hours; for example: placing a chair in a position, such as across an aisle, where a burglar would be likely to move it, or ringing up a certain amount on the cash register so that it might show evidence of being opened, as it is unlikely that a thief would ring up the same amount when he opened it. However, if an electric cash register is used and the current is turned off, the proprietor should be advised to leave it open as a burglar might damage the cash register by attempting to pry it open. It is never a good practice to leave money in a cash register over night.

If a police officer is to inform the merchants of the various schemes that might be used to victimize them, *it is essential that the officer have a good general knowledge of the methods of bad check artists, counterfeiters and confidence game operators.* There are at least three ways of gaining such knowledge. First, there is a great deal of material in book and pamphlet form. Your local Credit Bureau or Better Business Bureau will have much of this material on file and will be glad to loan it to you. Most libraries will have books on confidence games. The Secret Service has excellent publications on counterfeiting and forgery of government checks and securities that it will be happy to send police officers. Second, keep up on newspaper and magazine stories of these frauds. Remember that it is essential that persons making a living by fraud keep on the go, so they may soon be in your town and on your beat. Third, talk to older officers, officers from other towns and some of the more experienced business men in your community and let them tell you about con games that they know about personally.

When you start to study methods of check passers,

con men and counterfeiters, you will find that they all follow certain routine plans in their operations. All of these criminals will put new twists on their schemes, but you will recognize that they have just worked out a new angle for a fraud that has been used for years. Then, if you study these methods

Let your merchants know when forgers and frauds are operating

enough, you will be able to spot one of these deals just by knowing about a part of it. For example, if you hear that a well-dressed woman has just walked indignantly out of a store after refusing to make a purchase because the clerk took time to check a perfectly good $500 bill that she presented, you will know that in a short time the woman will be back in the store, apologize for her hasty action, accept her original purchase, give them a $500 bill and then be on her way before they find out that the second bill is counterfeit, even though the original was good. The public believes that police officers know about such things as these, and the public has a right to expect that they do.

Incidentally, the study of criminal methods does not apply to only those cases just cited. *One of the earmarks of a good officer is his interest in improving himself and his interest in learning more about police work.* The field of law enforcement is making rapid progress. If you are to keep up with this progress, you are going to have to do a lot of studying on the outside. It isn't just enough to put in the eight hours on your shift. If you are in a large police department, it will be easy to get material on police methods from your police academy or training division. If you are in a small police department, the job is more difficult but you can learn where to secure such material. Your Chief very probably will know sources of material. There may be a police training unit in your state college or university. Almost every large city in the country does have a good police training division now and you can visit them. Unfortunately, some of the best material in the police field is not in a written form. Much of it is still in the minds of the officers who learned it by actually performing the duties. However, more and more material is being put into written form so it is getting easier to find.

call on new-comers to the community

MAKE IT A POLICY *to call on new-comers to the community.* Let them know that the police are on the job. First impressions are always the most last-

Welcome new-comers to your community

ing. People who are new to the community always have many problems in getting settled and appreciate help. In turn, they can repay you by letting you

51

know promptly whenever they have information that might be of value. In addition, it will give you a good chance to look them over. You can get an idea of what kind of people they are going to be. You never know when this information will be of value.

make friends of people in a position to help

THERE ARE MANY CLASSES *of people who because of their occupations are particularly likely to be of value to the police. Cultivate their friendship as much as possible.* Milkmen, bread-truck men and paper boys all work early mornings when most people are in bed. They cover the entire town and have an excellent opportunity to observe all sorts of activities. Learn who these people are, call them by name. Their jobs are lonely and they appreciate any notice. Filling station attendants are another good source of information because much of our crime is associated with automobiles. They have a good chance to look a car over, they see how much money the driver is carrying, what is in the back seat, notice peculiarities in license plates, and other points of importance. Drop in the stations and talk to them, but stay out of the driveway in front of the pumps so as not to interfere with business. Night watchmen have a lot of time on their hands. They often observe activity of interest to the police. Drop by or work out a system of having them call the station to check in at intervals. Old people and children observe a great deal more than most people realize. Boys of about 12 or 13 can generally identify all makes and models of automobiles. Old people often sit out on front porches without much to do. They

Get to know people whose jobs give them a chance to observe

may give you valuable tips on things they have noticed if they regard you as a friend.

Inasmuch as many criminals are transient, get to know the hotel clerks, bell boys, rooming house operators and tourist camp owners. Few of them want criminals staying in their place. They are generally shrewd when it comes to sizing up a person and usually give his baggage and personal effects a good looking over.

Railroad crossing watchmen are often in a good position to observe activity. They are located on a main street and have much free time. It is a good practice to give them the descriptions of stolen cars. They will often check the passing traffic to pass the time faster. Cab drivers are another class that get around a lot. Often there is a great deal of friction between cab drivers and the police as taxis are always notorious traffic law violators. However, if they are treated fairly, but firmly, they are good sources of information. Once they learn that the laws are being enforced and that all cabs must obey them, they are more friendly. While some cab drivers are involved in petty criminal activity, most of them are honest and can be of great assistance.

You can repay these people by extending them your friendship. If you are a good, efficient and honest police officer, they will know it and they will be proud to be your friend and to be of assistance to you. In addition, there are certain small favors that you can legitimately do for them. While these are the same sorts of services that you would extend to every citizen, many people are reluctant to ask police officers for assistance. However, as you get to know these people, they will come to you for advice on all sorts of problems. Give them all the help you can. It is excellent public relations. You will not be able to do everything they ask or answer all their questions. If you can't answer the question, hunt up the answer for them if you can or tell them where they can find the answer. If you can't handle their request, explain why and give them all the help you can.

This whole field of public relations is so important that a separate text has been written on this subject alone. There has never been a successful police officer who was unable to get along with the public. While you can be a tough guy and get everybody sore at you and still make a lot of arrests, you are not doing the best possible police job. You can be plenty tough in the right kind of way and still have people like you.

improve your ability to observe

EVERYONE SEES *a street differently.* A salesman for breakfast food looks for the grocery stores, and an engineer looks at the construction of the street. A sailor looks for girls. A fireman looks for fire plugs, fire escapes, and hazards.

A policeman must look for many things. Far too many officers spend their time on patrol day-dreaming or being interested in something aside from police work. To do the best job, an officer must develop certain habits in observation that will aid him. Some of these habits are easy to develop, some are difficult, but once they have become automatic, they will always be there and save a great deal of effort in checking while on patrol.

One of the important things to remember when you are on patrol is that first of all you are a policeman. Second, you are a traffic officer, a vice squad officer, an auto theft detective or a juvenile officer. The point is, look for all violations of the law. As mentioned in the sections under traffic arrests, it may not always be advisable to make arrests in case of every violation. It may interfere with the job that you are assigned to do. As a result, some minor violations must be overlooked. However, there is a strong tendency for officers in the vice squad to be able to pick out a prostitute two blocks away but miss every drunken driver on the street unless one actually hits them. On the other hand, the traffic

You see the things you are most interested in

car can be patrolling and so long as a policy writer doesn't jaywalk he is perfectly safe so far as they are concerned. This isn't good police work. *Every time the public sees you overlook a violation, they lose some respect for the law.* They don't know that you are a specialized type of police officer. One of the big difficulties in the police field at present is this overspecialization. While it is necessary that police officers be specialized to a certain extent in order to work more efficiently, this can certainly be overdone. Don't let it happen to you. Remember that you are enforcing the law when you are out on the street.

Every time that you make a good arrest, ask yourself the question *"What tipped me off that something was wrong—what attracted my attention?"* You will generally find that it was some seemingly insignificant act or piece of evidence that first attracted you. It isn't easy to go back and determine just what made you suspicious. When you do, you will generally find that it was something very minor, just the way somebody turned around and looked at you a second or two too long, or the way that someone was moving a little too rapidly away from the door. Spend a little time talking this over with your partner and see just what it was that led you to some of your good arrests. When you do this, you will find that the rather vague feeling you get when you think something is wrong actually has a pretty firm foundation in your observation. Remember what these clues are and in the future look for similar situations on the street. *Experience as a police officer will be of value only if you continually try to improve your own ability.*

know the vehicles on the street

THERE IS A MOTOR VEHICLE of some sort involved in many crimes. A car or truck may be used either as a means of transportation to and from a crime scene or as a means of moving stolen property. One reason that our crime rate exceeds England's is simply because we have a larger country and transportation by automobile is so much more common. There, only persons with a considerable income can afford a car; the places to go are limited by the small size of the island. Taxes on a car in the Ford class in England were about $150 a year before the war. On the other hand, in this country, you could buy a used car (in normal times) for $150. There is little limit to the distance you can travel. A criminal perpetrating a hold-up in Ohio can be in Iowa the next morning—in Colorado that evening. In doing so, he has passed through six states with all of their various laws and officers including State Police, Highway Patrol, Sheriffs, Marshals, Constables, and City Police Officers.

The automobile has changed the entire criminal picture. At the start of this century a stranger stood out in a small town. His transportation was limited either to horse and buggy or to a train. As a result, there was not much travel. This made it difficult for a criminal to come into a town, pull a job, and then leave. One result was that any criminal going into a strange town was very likely to be a highly skilled

61

specialist in one particular criminal line. If he was a safe blower, all he did was blow safes. He might take some time in building up his job, do a good neat job, and get out of town successfully. This has all changed with the advent of the automobile. A stranger no longer stands out in any town in the

Check on drivers or passengers who look out of place

country. There is a constant stream of automobile and truck traffic on all of our highways. Now any punk who wants to steal a car or buy a car can pull any of a number of criminal jobs within a considerable radius of his home, and be assured of a reasonably certain getaway. The clever planning is no longer necessary. As a result, many types of crime have increased.

know the year, model and make of automobiles

BECAUSE OF THIS DIFFICULTY introduced by the automobile, *it is essential that police officers pay close attention to all motor vehicles.* A good officer will be able to determine the make, model and year of a car at a glance and from any angle. This is not easy to do. To develop the ability an officer must practice constantly. As much of the time as possible he should observe cars and look for the small details that show the differences. When two officers are working together, it is good practice for one of them to call out the make and year of cars they meet and for the other to check him. The problem is made more difficult because there are only minor differences in many of the cars made by the same manufacturer. The differences may be only in the radiator shell, bumpers, headlights, trim or tail-lights. For example, Chrysler makes the Plymouth, Dodge, DeSoto, and Chrysler; General Motors makes the Chevrolet, Pontiac, Oldsmobile, Buick, Cadillac and La Salle; Ford, the Ford, Mercury, Lincoln Zephyr, and Lincoln. Changes from year to year in a particular make are often limited to details without the over-all appearance of the car being altered.

In addition to knowing the differences between makes and models, *an officer should know license plates.* If the system is used, an officer should, as a minimum, know the designating numbers for all of the larger counties in the state as well as fifteen or twenty counties surrounding his own. He should be able to pick out the current license plates of adjoining states and the other out-of-state plates ordinarily encountered.

know regularly parked cars

AN OFFICER WILL FIND IT HELPFUL *to learn the cars ordinarily left for the night on his beat.* He should develop the habit of remembering them; then, whenever a car not usually left on his beat shows up, it will be noticed at once and can be checked. Trucks should have the same attention as passenger cars as they are often used, particularly panel models, by thieves.

It goes without saying that any car left with the motor running should be checked at once. This may be a get-away car in a hold-up. In any case, it is a violation of the law and a dangerous practice, both as a traffic hazard and as an invitation to someone, particularly a juvenile, to steal the car.

A car parked with the motor running is always worth
checking

be on the alert for traffic violations

A COMMON ERROR *made by officers patrolling is the failure to observe and make arrests or give warnings for traffic violations.* Many police officers feel that making a traffic arrest is beneath their dignity; others feel that it is the duty of men assigned to the traffic division (if the department is large enough to have such a division). In any case, failure to recognize traffic violations and failure to take the proper action is poor police work. All police officers in uniform should make traffic arrests for three reasons:

1. The traffic problem is the most serious problem now confronting the police. Many more persons are killed by traffic accidents than by criminals. Much more property is destroyed in traffic accidents than is lost to burglars, robbers, forgers and similar law breakers. The single most effective way to reduce the number of accidents is to arrest traffic law violators.

2. Making traffic arrests is good police work. Many criminals that would have otherwise escaped have been arrested because they violated a traffic law and were arrested by an alert officer. For example, a man in a stolen car who had committed an armed robbery and already escaped once from the police was arrested by a highway patrolman

after he had failed to dim his lights upon meeting
another car. Stopping a car for a traffic violation
gives the officers an excellent opportunity to look
over the car and the driver, check licenses and
question the driver briefly.

*3. Failure to observe and stop cars for traffic
violations is very poor public relations.* All drivers

Don't be too much of a big shot to make traffic arrests

notice police cars. If they commit a violation and
then see a police car, or if they see another driver
violate the law and no arrest follows, they gain a
very poor impression of law enforcement and the
police in general.

*The police officer should be thoroughly familiar
with the driver licensing laws and vehicle licensing*

laws of not only his own city and state, but also the adjoining states and other states whose vehicles he is likely to encounter. Many officers will believe that this is a useless requirement. They feel that these licensing restrictions have little relation to actual police work. This is a poor attitude to take. One of the major reasons why it is good police work to know these laws is based on the fact that a police officer has wide powers in stopping a vehicle and examining the driver for a license and also examining the registration of the vehicle. This allows you legally to make a quick investigation of suspicious persons that you would otherwise have no lawful right to stop and examine. It is common knowledge among police officers that a great many criminals do not have a proper driver's license or are driving an improperly-registered vehicle. Further, many law violators are driving vehicles that are improperly equipped, as for example, the tail-light may not be operating, brakes may be defective, or there may be some other violation of the equipment laws. A check of the driver's license and vehicle registration will not only uncover a number of these violations, but will give you a chance to look over both the driver and the vehicle.

Look up when you patrol or when you search

look up when you patrol

ONE GOOD HABIT *to develop is to look up. Observe above the first floor.* In one case two burglars repeatedly burglarized the same building and escaped by climbing down out of a third story window, with their loot, to the roof of a one story building. They could have been observed at any time. They made this one story climb between 11 and 12 at night. There was still considerable traffic on the street. The adjoining corner was a street car and bus transfer point; a large movie was just around the corner and lights from a filling station illuminated the wall they climbed down; yet, no one saw them make this climb although they did it at least a dozen times. Try to recall what the second floor of any downtown building looks like, or ask your friends to describe it. Incidentally, this is a pretty good thing to remember if you want to watch someone. If you can get up 8 or 10 feet in the air, your chances of being seen are very much less. You not only will have a better view from that location, but you are much more difficult to spot. One officer successfully "hid" simply by climbing up a pipe in the sprinkler system of a large warehouse. He was in full view but since he was about 10 feet in the air, a number of persons went directly underneath him and never noticed him.

A second good habit is to *look at the floors in stores.* Most burglars work fast. They will throw merchandise or papers they are not interested in on the floors. Often when a light is shown in a store, they will simply duck, perhaps lie on the floor, so look for them there. Make it a habit to look at every window to see if it is tightly closed. Learn to look *at* the glass, not through it. Often, if a window is broken out cleanly, it is not noticeable unless you have learned to observe for reflections in it. Look for disorder in display windows. A side glass not easily seen may have been broken.

look closely at doors and windows

CERTAIN TYPES OF BREAKS *in windows or door glass are particularly significant.* One common method of gaining entrance is to break the glass near the lock and then reach through and open the lock. Therefore, in the ordinary type of window, a break immediately above the lock should demand immediate attention. Many industrial windows are constructed of a number of small panes set in steel frames. As a general rule, the center section of this type of window is hinged so that it may be opened. The lock may be in any of several positions around this center section, so watch for breaks in that area. Be particularly careful to observe if an entire small pane is broken out. This may have been done so that no jagged edges remain to attract attention, or it may have been done to allow someone to enter directly through the break. It is always good practice for police officers to study the many different types of windows and window locks used in industrial buildings. They should learn the weakness of each type of window and lock and the points to look for in a rapid check to determine whether or not the window has been used as a means of entrance.

Be particularly observant of display windows. It is easy enough to observe when a thief breaks the large front display window to get out valuable merchandise, but very often there will be smaller side windows that are much more difficult to see.

Watch for the small signs that indicate a burglary

They can also be broken with less noise. As a result, then, these are the type that the thieves generally pick. Breaks in any display window are not difficult to observe and should never be missed by an officer on foot when they are on the same side of the street he is patrolling. However, they are difficult to spot across the street or from an automobile. One of the best things to look for is reflections in the glass. Look at these windows often enough so that you know what sort of reflections to expect. If you see the reflection isn't there it is a good chance the glass isn't there either. Usually a thief taking merchandise from a display window will leave the window in considerable disorder. That is one of the quick ways to spot a break. However, it isn't always easy to see that the things are out of order if the items are generally small, as for example, a jewelry store window. As a result, you must use a great deal of care in making these observations. There is nothing that reflects more on a police officer than to have him fail to be the first to discover a break-in. It is only right to expect that if he doesn't catch the thief in the act, he at least discovers the break-in before the owner comes down and unlocks the next morning.

There are a number of marks that might be left in a break-in. If a jimmy is used in opening an ordinary residence window, the marks will usually be found between the sill and the lower sash at about the center. The reason for this is that the burglar is attempting to apply enough pressure either to break the window lock or pull out the screws holding it. To do this without breaking the window, it is necessary that he apply his pressure so that the force is equal on each side of the frame of the sash. Jimmy marks on a door will ordinarily be found near the lock as force is best exerted at this point. However, there are a number of other methods of opening a door. One method is to remove the pins from the hinges. In good construction, the pins in the hinges of an exterior door will either be on the inside of the door, hidden in the construction or welded into place. However, in the case of interior doors or cheap construction, these pins may be removed easily. The burglar may then enter, unlock the door from the inside and then replace the pins while he works inside. The best thing to look for here is the presence of tool marks on the pins. Another method of entry used on doors padlocked shut is to put a bar through the hasp and then pry it off, pulling the screws from the wood. As the burglar is leaving, he may push the screws back in and the lock will appear normal to a casual observer. However, because of the force necessary, the bar used will leave marks on the door frame. In addition, almost any movement of the padlock will show that the hasp is loose. An exceptionally clever method that has been used is applied to cylinder type locks. In many of these locks, the cylinder holding the tumblers is screwed into the lock mechanism from the outside of the door. A set screw is then put in place so that it will keep the cylinder from revolving and being unscrewed. However, some burglars have been successful in applying enough force to the cylinder with a wrench placed on the projecting rim of the cylinder to break this set screw and allow the lock to be unscrewed. It is then a simple matter to reach in with a screwdriver

Some smart burglars use this
method

or similar tool, unlock the door, replace the cylinder and go in the building. In some cases, careless locksmiths have failed to replace the set screws making it possible for the cylinder to be unscrewed with a minimum of force. As a result, officers on patrol should examine cylinder locks carefully for tool marks and take immediate action if they discover marks, assuming until they find otherwise that the burglar is still in the building, even though the door is now securely locked.

Remember, there are other ways of gaining entrance to a building than through the doors or windows. For example, there may be sidewalk openings. Many stores get their coal or oil supplies through a manhole set out near the curb. Very often these manholes are not properly secured. It is only the work of a few seconds to lift this cover, drop in and then either put the cover in place or have a confederate put it in place. A great many business places also have entrances to the basement leading directly out on to the sidewalk. This is usually a door flush with the sidewalk. Again, it is often inconvenient to lock these doors and very often employees will forget to check them before closing for the night. Many business buildings have air shafts from the basement leading up to the sidewalk. These shafts will be covered by a grating set in the sidewalk. Such grating is not always set permanently into the sidewalk so may be removed entirely or a small section may be removed. Presence of this grating gives the store owner a false sense of security so you will find that these basement windows are not locked in the usual manner. Again, here is a very weak point. These same types of openings, of course, will also occur at the sides or at the rear of the business buildings. As a result, you have to do a lot of looking around. That is exactly what a burglar will do.

The occupants of many older buildings will forget that there may be an unused door giving direct access from the adjoining building. Such openings frequently occur in basements but may occur on any floor of the building. As a result, if they are not securely locked, entrance into the building will be easy.

observe individuals

MODERN POLICE OFFICERS *are losing the art of identifying individuals from descriptions or mug photos.* Part of this ability to pick up criminals by sight is inborn, but much of it is learned and any police officer can improve his own ability if he makes an effort. It is unfortunate that there is so little written on this important subject, but an alert police officer can work out his own methods. He will soon learn that the ear is the single best feature to use for identification. There are more variations in the ears of individuals than in any other single feature and study will soon develop the ability to see and recognize these differences. Other facial characteristics often overlooked are the hairline, type of nose, profile and spacing and condition of teeth.

Practice describing people in your own mind at a glance. Learn to estimate weight, height, and age. Practice looking for points that make one person different from another. In any town there are probably hundreds of men 5′9″, 165, dark hair, medium complexion, grey hat and dark suit. Look for such things as glasses, peculiarities in walking, objects being carried. Condition of clothing is always important, but seldom mentioned. For instance, a man described as above could be dressed conservatively or dressed like a tramp with clothes worn and dirty.

Good police officers greatly improve their abilities

to describe individuals by practicing as they drive down the street. One of the officers will suddenly say to the other, "Describe that man standing on the corner." With practice, you not only develop the habit of working up a graphic mental description of almost everyone you see, but you will be able to get a very accurate description with only a glance

No two people look alike. Look for the differences

at the individual. You will soon find that your ability to describe persons has improved much more than you ever thought possible.

As a police officer the greatest part of your work is with human beings. Your ability to describe them rapidly and easily and tell one from the other is as important as any other ability that you can develop.

Instead of just wasting your time when you are riding around in a squad car, you might as well be developing this ability. It is a long hard process to become a good police officer. You must take advantage of every opportunity. By observing individuals closely and developing descriptions of them, you will not only be doing good police work, you will be improving yourself.

suspicious persons

CERTAIN OFFICERS *are very successful in appre-hending criminals on the street.* They seem to have a special sense that tells them "that man is wrong." Many of these officers believe they have a special endowment while others, equally successful, who have analyzed their ability find that they have learned to look for certain points that often distin-guish a criminal. They have learned to observe de-tails of dress, action and appearance, details often so minor that they have no meaning in themselves but only when observed in connection with other points.

It is difficult to set rules to follow in developing this ability and hard to list the points to observe. Much will depend upon the intelligence of the officer and his careful and thoughtful application to his job. However, to an able law enforcement officer, briefly mentioning the techniques and points to observe used by certain officers will suggest ways of improving his own ability.

The basic rule is: *Look for the differences;* the unusual acts, methods of dress or ways of doing things that may set a criminal apart from the ordi-nary citizen. For example, a person who pays too much attention to you, watches your every move, notices which way you turn, might bear watching. On the other hand, a person who seems to avoid you, acts as though you were not there, is indifferent to an extreme, has set himself apart. Of course, this alone does not mean the man has just broken jail, but it is an indication. As an example, an employee of a certain company who was unusually friendly to police, going out of his way to greet them very cordially, was discovered in the theft of a large number of valuable cameras.

There are other points. *In observing traffic, notice drivers who are not familiar with the operation of the car,* have difficulty shifting, skid the wheels suddenly when making a routine stop, or stall the motor. If the driver is a woman, this does not indicate a great deal; it is too routine. However, if the driver is a man, particularly a young man, you have a good prospect as an auto thief. Watch him for a while. Some officers even let a suspicious person in a car know he is being followed, then watch to see what he does. He may be using the rear view mirror constantly to observe you; he may stall along to see if you will pass him; he may turn off. It is good practice, if you believe the car is stolen because the driver is watching you so carefully, or seeking to avoid you, to drive up beside him suddenly as though you were going to stop him and see what he does. He may jump out and run, he may try to outrun you in the car. If he does neither, you can drop back. You will not have lost anything. An honest citizen will rarely notice you, but you can be sure a car thief will.

Always note persons who are loitering. There are certain areas where people normally congregate, on

A car thief may not be familiar with the operation of the
car

corners or in front of stores for example, visiting and observing passers-by. There are many more areas where this does not occur, as there is little of interest; where few stores are open and persons usually walk as though they had a definite destination in mind. Here again a person or persons strolling along set themselves apart and should be noticed. The greater part of the time, this activity will mean nothing unusual; on the other hand, it will occasionally. Thus, it is well worth police interest. Again, two or more persons slowly walking through an area where there is apparently little of interest and who are not talking to each other is unusual. Watch them, see what they are looking at, how long they remain in the area, how much notice they take of you, whether or not they select a route that brings them past the same point several times. All of these facts may be significant.

Remember that a great many criminals use a lookout while they work. The criminal himself may be well out of sight, down in the basement of a building or in some other location where it would be difficult to notice him from the street. However, his lookout may be in plain view. The lookout has to be where he can see you, and if he can see you, there is always a chance that you can see him. He may appear to be only someone loitering in the neighborhood. On the other hand, he may be partly concealed or may suddenly jump back into a doorway as you approach. As a result, whenever you do observe a suspicious person, do not immediately assume that he is the criminal. He may be just the lookout. If you do stop and question such a suspicious person it is always well to look around the neighborhood to make sure that there is no criminal activity. A lookout isn't going to want you to do this. He may try to divert your attention by attempting to escape or some such statement as "Let's get going and get this thing over with." Watch for this sort of activity. Observe such things as whether or not he keeps looking at one particular place. While many of the suspicious persons that you do question will not be part of a general criminal operation, it does occur often enough so that you should always watch for this possibility. Remember that very few crimes are broken open all at once. The solution of a great many offenses starts when some alert police officer notices some little thing. This acts as a wedge in breaking the crime open. It leads to some additional point and pretty soon enough material is accumulated to solve a crime.

Remember in patrolling that certain areas are particularly appropriate for certain types of crimes; so in those areas concentrate your observation on the indications of the type of offense peculiar to the area. For example, around bus and railroad depots look for persons with luggage that is obviously of too good quality for them to carry. Watch for travellers being accosted by persons whom they do not appear to know; many of the best confidence games operate around depots. Look for boys and girls who appear to be unfamiliar with the town;

they might be run-aways. Certain areas, generally residential, are often set-ups for purse-snatchers, particularly if the streets are not well-lighted. Watch for boys or younger active men who do not appear to have a definite destination. In similar areas, bur-

Watch for anything that looks out of place

glars may be active, so hit the alleys, look for cars parked in front of vacant lots or in locations not conveniently accessible to a house. In short, study where crimes are occurring in the area you patrol, then look for that type of crime in the area where it is most likely to be found. In addition, try to study the type of people who are committing crimes in your area. This will lead to some interesting conclusions. You may find that almost all the crimes on your beat are committed by persons living outside of your beat or that a high proportion of crimes are committed by persons who use automobiles to get into your beat or you may find that many of the criminals are of a particular race. You will normally observe many of these things, but your observations are not always accurate unless you keep written records of what goes on. Most police officials will be glad to help you make a study of your particular beat. Any good Chief wants to see his patrolmen do the best possible job.

use of spotlight

THE PROPER USE *of a spotlight from a police car at night is valuable.* The best type of spotlight is the kind that is attached to a cord and operated from the car battery. This type can be flashed around much more easily than the fixed type operated by a

Use your spotlight properly

knob from inside the car. There isn't any good all around spotlight for use in police work. In any case, no matter what sort of equipment you do have, get so that you can use it properly. Know just what your spotlight will do and just how you can move it around. It is a pleasure to watch an officer who can really use a spotlight, work. You will find that there are two rules that you should follow:

The first rule is:

Use the light as little as possible. Do not shine it around at random. Know where you should look at each building and hit these points rapidly. You might shine it in a store at the floor, the cash register and the safe, then up to the second floor for a quick sweep, then shut it off.

The second rule is:

Do not shine the light up and down a street as you move it across. It may be seen for a long distance. Shut it off. Some types have a trigger type switch that is very convenient for this.

emergency calls

DON'T GO IN ON AN EMERGENCY CALL *unless you are actually sent.* In a great many cities you will see that almost every emergency is cluttered up with useless police cars and police officers who came along just for the ride. They aren't doing anybody any good. Another point to remember is that if you need to use your siren for a right-of-way, determine a safe route so that you will not run into other police, fire or ambulance equipment. There have been a number of serious accidents where two vehicles, both with the siren wide open, have collided. You should know what the fire and ambulance routes are. They will almost invariably use the same route in going to a certain location. The police department should have a system worked up to avoid such danger. One way is to have the dispatcher say, "Calling Car 201—emergency." As soon as car 201 hears the word "emergency" they will respond, "Car 201. 10th and Main." The dispatcher will come back and say, "Car 201. Emergency from 10th and Main to 20th and Oak—the ambulance is on the way." Other radio equipped vehicles dispatched into the scene will then know the route that the police car is taking. Remember that the siren sounds loud to you in your car, but it doesn't necessarily mean that the public is going to give you the right-of-way. While many police departments have educated the public to respect a siren, this is not true everywhere. Windows rolled up in the winter time, the car radio on, and the heater and the defroster going will make it almost impossible to hear a siren. It is best to use it and then to drive as though you weren't using it at all. A red light will give you more help than most sirens. This is particularly true if the light is mounted high up on the car and is one of the oscillating types so it can be seen from any angle and will easily attract attention.

In any case, remember that *the main thing is to get to the scene safely*. If you go too fast, you may not get there at all. You should never use your siren and your red light unless there is an actual emergency. It doesn't do a police department any good to see a couple of cowboys in a squad car go tearing down the street, running around street cars on the wrong side and then throwing on the brakes and skidding for half a block up to a $10 property damage accident.

Every emergency call presents a different problem. No two are alike. However, there are certain general rules that will be of assistance in handling all emergency calls.

The first rule is:

    Treat all such calls as though an emergency actually existed. The largest number of such calls will be false alarms caused by a defective alarm, an excited person, or some similar circumstance. In many cases where a crime has actually occurred, the criminals will already be in flight. Do not as-

Treat every alarm like an actual emergency

sume this. Use all the care and caution you can in every case. Because you have made a run to a bank on an average of once a month simply because a scrub-woman has bumped an alarm switch with her mop, do not assume that this is the case.

It may get you killed and allow the offenders to escape.

The second rule is:

On hold-up and burglar or prowler calls, go in fast but quietly. Avoid the use of the siren and the red light so as not to warn the criminal. In assault cases, it might be advisable to use the siren in the hope that the assault might be stopped and the victim saved from further injury. This policy will vary with individual circumstances. For example, in an assault where the officer was nearby when he received the call, it might be best to go in quietly as the time would be so short there would be a minimum of injury to the victim.

The third rule is:

In going in on any case, avoid driving down the street where the call is located. A lookout might spot the police car some distance away. If at all possible, drive down a parallel street, turning at the last possible intersection.

The fourth rule is:

Always watch for persons escaping when driving up to any crime scene. Much of the time you will arrive after the offenders have left. Try to get them on your way in. If they are smart and leave the scene casually and at a reasonable speed, you may not spot them, but frequently they will lose their

Remember that a lookout may be watching for you

heads and run from the scene or drive off at a high speed, disregarding traffic laws.

Many cases have been solved in a few minutes because an officer on the way in took time to observe persons or automobiles.

The fifth rule is:

Upon arriving at the scene, do not rush into any activity. Take time to size up the situation. This may require only fifteen or twenty seconds, but all too often officers will jump out of a car and run up

Be alert as you go in to the scene, you may catch them escaping

to a house or store when, if they had taken time to observe, they might have seen the criminal running off in the opposite direction or noticed an armed lookout in a car.

The sixth rule is:

Have a general plan beforehand. A poor plan is better than no plan at all. Even the simplest planning is effective. For example, some teams of officers agree beforehand that on all burglar calls where there is an alley, the officer not driving will

be dropped out of the car in the alley and the
driver will run the car around to the front of the
building and go up to the front door in the chance
he will frighten the offender out the back way
where he will be apprehended. Where there is no
alley, the car will pull up in front and the first officer will run at once to the rear, and the driver will

Have a plan of action laid out

take the front. These plans must be varied with the
individual circumstances, but the substance of the
plan is that the first officer out of the car takes the
back of the place, the second the front.

Sometimes this may be reversed. For example, in a
business district, it may be simpler for the first

officer to drop out in front of the place of business while the driver runs the car around into the alley. In any case, the two officers do not get out of the car together and walk up to the front door.

There are exceptions to this rule, however. As previously pointed out, it is essential that all officers have a full knowledge of buildings so if there is no back entrance to a small store, but if there is a sky-light, both officers may get out together and one take the front door while the other covers the sky-light and roof.

As a general rule in hold-up calls, the first officer will cover the front door and the second officer block escapes. Blocking the escape may mean block-ing a side entrance or apprehending the driver of the get-away car.

In the cases where an officer is working alone and on foot, the best general practice in burglaries is to approach from the rear of the building, or if the point of entrance is known, from that side of the building. It is seldom that aid can be secured in such cases in time to block other points of escape. Further action on the part of the officer will depend upon the circumstances of the individual case. Under certain conditions, the best thing to do would be to wait for the burglar to come out. Again, particu-larly if the officer believed his presence were known, it might be best to go on in, using the methods sug-gested in the section on searching buildings.

Two other general practices are of value. One is to *have a simple set of flashlight signals to avoid shouting and so warning a criminal.* The usual signals are:

> 1 flash —here I am
> 2 flashes—come here
> 3 flashes—hold your position

In the daylight the first signal would not be needed, the second would be to motion as in motioning traffic on, and the third, holding the hand palm towards the other officer as in stopping traffic. In communicating over distances, those signals may be given by whistle, or in an emergency, by gun fire or auto horns.

The second general practice is used in cases where officers have been assigned to the front and rear of a building to prevent an intruder from escaping. In such a case the *officers should take opposite corners of the building.* This will allow an officer to see two sides of a building while his partner sees the other two sides. In case of gun fire, they are out of each other's line of fire. The simplest rule is to "keep to the right,"—that is, stand at the right hand corner of the building as you face it.

In blocking escape, it is sometimes necessary to disable an automobile quickly. In doing this, first look for the keys. They may have been left in the lock. If they have been, all you need to do is jerk them out and keep them. If they are not there, the easiest thing to do is lift the hood and jerk the ignition wires loose. If you have a little more time, take off or break the top of the distributor. There are many other ways to disable a car, such as shooting out a tire, shooting into the gas tank or radiator, but the ignition system is the weakest point, so best attacked.

After arriving at a location and blocking means of escape, further action will depend on the circumstances. There are several points to be remembered here.

Take opposite corners to cover a building

First: Determine if it is a false alarm. Be cautious here. Simply because a bank employee steps out and waves you on, do not assume that everything is all right; someone may be holding a gun in his back. There is a case where a team of officers arriving at the scene of a hold-up call believed everything looked in order. The store had a large show window and was well-lit, so that they could see the interior of the store. Several people were standing together in the store and appeared to be in conversation. One of the officers went to inquire about the call. One

Make sure that an emergency doesn't actually exist

of the persons in the group suddenly raised a gun he had been holding at his side and shot and killed the officer. This presents a problem. Obviously, it would not have been good policy to have called assistance and surrounded this seemingly innocent store, nor would it have been wise to go in with drawn guns where everything seemed peaceful. Although this is the sort of case that rarely occurs, it should not be disregarded. Therefore, make it a practice to stay alert, even though there appears to be no actual crime.

Do not let down until you are certain of the situation.

Second: It is a good practice to stay away from groups. Call people over to you one at a time. This gives you a chance to look them over as they approach. Get in a position so that you are protected from the back, either by your partner or a solid wall of some sort. Here again is a situation where it is important to know the owner of a business or a key employee. If possible, get an OK from one of them when you go in on a hold-up.

Third: What should you do if you discover a hold-up actually is in process? The answer will depend upon the circumstances of each case, such as the number of people in the place of business, possible escape routes, the character of the hold-up man (insofar as you can judge), and your own ability with a gun.

Remember that the protection of life comes before the protection of property. Therefore, avoid any situation where citizens might be injured or killed by gun-fire. Also, consider your own safety. As a general rule, do not put yourself in a dangerous position unless it is necessary to protect someone else. This does not mean to avoid contact with a criminal. Often the fact that a police officer goes right in after him will cause the hold-up man to drop his gun. The best combination is common sense and bravery. Most of the time you will have an advantage. The majority of police officers are better armed than the usual criminal; the officer is not seeking to escape so can choose his position; he has more experience than the criminal and more courage. Use

Don't catch the public in your crossfire

these advantages. It looks well in the papers to rush in with guns blazing and capture a criminal, but it looks very bad to rush in and shoot, or have the criminal shoot, an innocent bystander.

In assault cases where a criminal is actually doing harm to a citizen, the officer has no choice but to go in at once. Here you can operate on the theory that a good attack is the best defense. Take advantage of cover and protect yourself, but go in fast. However, do not be foolhardy. If you know, for example, that a criminal in an apartment has already killed the occupant, it is foolish to go in after him. Block his escape and drive him out with gas or other means.

search of buildings for prowlers

HERE AGAIN, as in all police work, *the action taken will depend upon the circumstances*. The following steps are intended only as general guides.

First: Cut off escape. Get help if necessary. It is foolish to start into a building if it is easily possible for the intruder to slip out. In some circumstances you may not be able to get aid. Whether or not you go into the building, leaving points of possible escape unguarded will depend on the circumstances of the case. For example, if you believe the intruder does not know you are there, go in, carefully and quietly. If he knows you are there, do your best to block escape. If there are so few ways of escape that you can watch them from inside the building, it might be best to go in. Consider misleading the criminal into believing you are in the building when actually you are at a point outside where you can cover the exits.

Second: Be systematic in a search. Do not go hit and miss. When you search an area, search it so well you will not need to return to it. This does not mean to go to extremes, such as climbing through small openings or moving heavy objects, but rather to avoid trying one or two rooms on one floor, then running to the basement for a quick look and then up to the second floor.

Third: When you open a door to a room, stand out of line of any possible fire from the room, then

106

Cover the exits before you start a search

Don't try to search everywhere at once

*slam the door back hard so as to hit anyone con-
cealed behind the door.* When you go in a door,
particularly at night, and if it is darker in the room
than on the outside, go in fast and then step to one
side with your back to the wall. This will avoid being framed against the light any longer than necessary.

*Fourth: When you leave a room close the door
and leave the light on.* If you can, lock the door.
This is to prevent anyone from moving into a room
you have already searched.

Fifth: Look up in searches. A criminal may hide
on top of a bookcase, stock rack, or tall piece of
furniture.

Slam the doors back—Keep your flashlight
away from your body

Sixth: Keep your flash light out of your gun hand and away from your body. It makes a good target.

Seventh: It is difficult to make a set statement about whether or not to draw your gun on a search. In any case, have it ready. If your holster has a flap or safety strap, get it unstrapped and out of the way, and lift your gun in the holster and let it drop back so you know it is loose. If you believe you should have your gun out of the holster, observe two rules: 1. Do not cock it. 2. Keep your thumb clear of the hammer so as not to interfere with the double action.

Eighth: If it is necessary for a citizen to accompany you as a guide, have him stay in back of you and a few feet away. This is for two reasons: First, you do not want him in the most dangerous position, and second, you do not want him in such a position as to prevent you from shooting. Unless it is necessary, do not allow citizens to accompany you —they only cause trouble. However, it is a good plan to have someone who can identify persons lawfully within the building, easily available.

two situations in which to use caution

IN THOSE SITUATIONS that will require police action, the usual practice for a uniformed officer is to go right ahead and make the arrest or take whatever action he believes necessary to handle the problem properly. There are two situations in particular where more than usual caution is advisable before taking any action. While what you do will be determined by the policy of your local department, in the cases of stolen cars or narcotic addicts, *it is not always best to search the car or attempt an arrest immediately.* Inexperienced police officers upon observing a stolen car parked without anyone in it will immediately go up to the car and start checking it over to make sure it is the one they want. This is never a good practice unless you are absolutely certain that the car has been abandoned. For example, a car sitting in a snow drift and covered so that it looks as if it has been there for a matter of days would probably be safe to check immediately. In many other cases the person who stole the car might be just ready to go out and get in. The shorter the time the car has been stolen, the more important this point is. If you do see a stolen car parked on the street, appear to disregard it but get in a position to watch it. If you are a member of a large department that has a detective division, you should call in for assistance from this division. As they aren't in uniform they will be in a much better position to watch this car without any fear of discovery. In any case, you should report finding this car immediately through the use of your radio system and then wait for further instructions. Your commanding officers may have determined that this car was stolen by joyriders who will not return to the car. On the other hand, they already may have the car under observation. The point to remember is, stay away from this stolen car until you know what you should do about it. When you are instructed to approach a stolen car do not go right up and start rummaging through it. You may destroy fingerprints or other means of identification that the thief has left in the car. Use caution there.

You should use care in dealing with all narcotic addicts and all persons involved in the sale of narcotics. Most narcotic addicts and practically every small time narcotic salesman is already known to the law enforcement officers who are working on narcotics. Unless you know what you are doing, it is best to leave these fellows alone but turn over any information you have to the men who have specialized in narcotics. The reason for this is that these small time operators are only one link in a very complex system of distribution of narcotics. The men who are closely associated with the investigation of narcotics are interested in them only because they will lead them to one person nearer the source of supply. The small time addict may be six or seven steps away from the person who actually controls the supply of narcotics in your town or state. The only way you can get to this top man is through the small timer who leads you to a small time salesman who in turn lead them to a small time distributor who will finally go on up the scale to the top man. As a result, the best narcotic officers will know a great many violators but will not arrest them until they have gone up as near the top as they can. *Very good narcotics men may go for a year without making any arrests and still be doing difficult and successful police work for the entire time.* If you snatch some small time peddler, you may break up a case they have been working on for months. Know the situation in your town in relation to the sale of narcotics and be guided by it. If you are operating in a small town you may have to take direct action in some cases. Even then, there is doubtless an agency in your state that can give you a lot of help in handling these people. But remember this general principle, the small time narcotics violator is important largely because he can lead you to the man at the top. Determine before you make an arrest whether or not it will interfere with any investigations under way. This system of operation does not always apply. You will find that there are certain narcotics violators who depend quite largely upon theft for their supply. These fellows, of necessity, are on the go all the time. They may be attached to a carnival, small circus, or some other sort of job that lets them move rapidly from town to town. Instead of buying their supply they will steal it by breaking into doctor's offices, drug stores, veterinarian offices, or other places where they get their drug. In these cases, you can generally go ahead and take immediate action without breaking up any other investigation that is under way.

a final word of advice

THIS BOOK was intended to tell you some things about doing a good patrol job. But there isn't any book or series of books that can tell you all you need to know about being a good police officer. There are just too many things to learn. Some things you will learn only from experience. Whether or not you do learn them will depend upon how hard you are trying. Every time you get through handling a police situation, if you will go back over it in your mind and see where you did a good job or where you did a poor job, you will help yourself a great deal. You can *learn to avoid your mistakes* and you can *learn to repeat the things that you did well*.

Remember that you can learn much from older officers. Most of the material in this book was gained by observing older officers in the police field and watching how they worked. There is no substitute for this experience. This publication can only be a very general guide to you. Your position as a police officer is one of great public responsibility. You can do it well only if you make every attempt to learn all that you can about being a good police officer. The police field is rapidly changing. There are more and more opportunities presenting themselves. By learning to do the best possible job, you will be ready for these opportunities when they occur.